YOU CAN FOLLOW RULES

CHEAT OR PLAY FAIR?

You Choose the Ending

by Connie Colwell Miller • illustrated by Victoria Assanelli

Do you ever wish you could change a story or choose a different ending?

IN THESE BOOKS, YOU CAN!

Read along and when you see this:

WHAT HAPPENS NEXT?

Skip to the page for that choice, and see what happens.

In this story, Kirsten wants to win at Hide-and-Seek. Will she play fair or will she cheat? YOU make the choices!

Kirsten and her sister Mira are playing Hide-and-Seek. Kirsten lost. She really wants to win. But her sister always finds the best hiding spots!

"One, two, three . . ." Kirsten counts while Mira hides.

WHAT HAPPENS NEXT?

If Kirsten peeks, turn the page.
If Kirsten plays fair, turn to page 20.

Kirsten peeks through her fingers. Her sister is headed toward the kitchen. "Nine, ten! Ready or not, here I come!" Kirsten says.

Kirsten runs to the kitchen. She finds her sister in just a few seconds.

"Kirsten, did you peek?" Mira asks.

WHAT HAPPENS NEXT?

→ If Kirsten lies to her sister, turn the page.
If Kirsten tells the truth, turn to page 16. ←

"No," Kirsten lies. Now it's her turn to hide. "Ready or not, here I come!" yells Mira. As soon as she hears her sister coming, Kirsten thinks about switching spots.

WHAT HAPPENS NEXT?

→ If Kirsten sneaks to a new spot, turn the page.
If Kirsten plays fair and stays put, turn to page 12. ←

While Mira isn't looking, Kirsten sneaks past her and finds a new hiding spot.

After a few minutes, Mira calls out, "Kirsten, where are you? I've looked everywhere."

TURN THE PAGE →

9

Kirsten jumps out of her hiding spot. "Ha-ha!
You didn't find me! I win!"

"You're cheating!" Mira shouts. "I looked in that
spot already! I quit. I don't want to play with a cheater."

Kirsten is upset. She wanted to win so badly that she didn't play fair. And now her sister won't play with her anymore.

THE END

Go to page 23.

Kirsten stops and thinks about the rules of the game. If she switches spots, that's cheating again. She stays where she is hiding. Mira finds her quickly.

TURN THE PAGE →

13

Kirsten is a little disappointed that her sister found her already.

"Let's play again," Mira says. "It's your turn to count."

Kirsten decides to play fair without cheating for the rest
of the game. Playing with her sister is more fun than winning.

THE END

→ Go to page 23. ←

Kirsten tells the truth. "Yes," she says. "I'm sorry, Mira. I peeked. I just wanted to win so much!"

"Kirsten!" her sister complains. "That's not fair! I don't want to play with a cheater."

TURN THE PAGE →

"I know, Mira," Kirsten says. "I'm really sorry.
Will you still play with me?
Mira thinks for a minute, "Okay," she says.
"But no more cheating!"

Kirsten agrees to play fair, and the sisters play a few more games of Hide-and-Seek before dinner.

THE END

→ Go to page 23. ←

Kirsten really wants to win, but she knows she should play fair. She covers her eyes and finishes counting. "Ready or not, here I come!" She looks everywhere, but she can't find Mira.

Kirsten is just about to give up looking when she finds her sister! "Wow! Good spot, Mira!" Kirsten says.

TURN THE PAGE →

The girls keep playing all afternoon. They each win a few games. Kirsten thinks that winning while playing fair feels great. And losing is okay sometimes, if she's having fun with her sister.

THE END

THINK AGAIN

- What choices did you make for Kirsten? How did that story end?

- Go back to page 3. Read the story again and pick different choices. How did the story change?

- Have you ever cheated in a game? What happened?

Winning feels good. We all want to win, but rules matter. If you played a game, would YOU play fair or cheat?

For the real-life Mira and Kirsten who inspired this story.—C.C.M. & R.G.

AMICUS ILLUSTRATED and AMICUS INK
are published by Amicus
P.O. Box 1329, Mankato, MN 56002
www.amicuspublishing.us

Library of Congress Cataloging-in-Publication Data
Names: Miller, Connie Colwell, 1976- author. | Assanelli, Victoria, 1984-
  illustrator.
Title: You can follow rules : cheat or play fair? / by Connie Colwell
  Miller ; illustrated by Victoria Assanelli.
Description: Mankato, Minnesota : Amicus, [2020] | Series: Making good
  choices | Audience: K to Grade 3.
Identifiers: LCCN 2018033018 (print) | LCCN 2018050216 (ebook) | ISBN
  9781681517728 (pdf) | ISBN 9781681516905 (library binding) | ISBN
  9781681524764 (pbk.)
Subjects: LCSH: Sports--Moral and ethical aspects--Juvenile literature. |
  Sportsmanship--Juvenile literature. | Hide-and-seek--Juvenile literature.
  | Plot your own stories--Juvenile literature.
Classification: LCC GV706.3 (ebook) | LCC GV706.3 .M54 2020 (print) | DDC
  796.01--dc23
LC record available at https://lccn.loc.gov/2018033018

Editor: Rebecca Glaser
Series Designer: Kathleen Petelinsek
Book Designer: Veronica Scott

Printed in the United States of America
HC 10 9 8 7 6 5 4 3 2 1
PB 10 9 8 7 6 5 4 3 2 1

ABOUT THE AUTHOR

Connie Colwell Miller is a writer, editor, and instructor who lives in Mankato, Minnesota, with her four children. She has written over 100 books for young children. She likes to tell stories to her kids to teach them important life lessons.

ABOUT THE ILLUSTRATOR

Victoria Assanelli was born during the autumn of 1984 in Buenos Aires, Argentina. She spent most of her childhood playing with her grandparents, reading books, and drawing doodles. She began working as an illustrator in 2007, and has illustrated several textbooks and storybooks since.